Theory & Model Building In Social Work:

Course Materials

ALSO BY JANE GILGUN

Children's Books

Busjacked!
Emma and her Forever Person
Five Little Cygnets Cross the Bundoran Road
Patrick and the Magic Mountain
The King's Toast
The Little Pig Who Didn't go to Market
The Picking Flower Garden
Thorns Have Roses: A Story of Recovery from Clergy Abuse
Turtle Night at Playa Grande
Will the Soccer Star

Books

Child Sexual Abuse: From Harsh Realities to Hope
Children with Serious Conduct Issues
Hannah Robinson: The Celebrated Beauty of Her Day
I Want to Show You: Poems
On Being a Sh*t: Unkind Deeds & Cover-Ups in Everyday Life
The Logic of Murderous Rampages & Other Essays
on Violence & Its Prevention
The NEATS: A Child & Family Assessment

Manuals

Lemons or Lemonades? An Anger Workbook for Kids
Leomons or Lemonade? An Anger Workbook for Teens
Readiness to Adopt Children with Special Needs
The CASPARS: Clinical Assessment Tools for Client
Risks & Strengths

Jane Gilgun is a professor and writer. She has many books, articles, and assessment tools available through on-line bookstores and social media websites.

Theory & Model Building in Social Work

Course Materials

JANE F. GILGUN, PHD, LICSW

Createspace

Gilgun, Jane F.
Theory & Model Building in Social Work:
Course Materials

The essays in this book have appeared in e-bookstores such as Kindle,
Barnes & Noble, Apple iPad, Scribd.com, and Smashwords.

Cover Photo by Ellen Lodge
Glenade Lake, County Leitrim, Ireland

1.Ttheory and model building in social work
2. Social work education
3. Intervention research 4. Evidence-based practice
5. Grounded Theory
6. Deductive Qualitative Analysis 7. Research

ISBN-13: 978-1481805896
ISBN-10: 1481805894

Createspace

Visit Amazon Kindle, Google Books, iBooks,
& other Internet booksellers
to discover other books, articles, and children's stories
by Jane Gilgun that you may enjoy.

FOREWORD

This document is a collection of materials for the course, theory and model building in social work that I taught at the University of Minnesota, Twin Cities, USA, School of Social Work in the fall of 2012. Theory and modeling building is of high interest to social work researchers. Social workers have chosen a most demanding profession. Not only have we social taken on the tasks of trying to understand the most serious social problems of our time, but we also have chosen to take actions to contribute to the social good. The values of justice, care, dignity and respect of persons, and freedom underlie social work's commitment to understanding social issues and actions meant to respond to them.

We cannot be "headless machines," to quote Edith Abbott, one of the founding mothers of social work. Effective social work builds upon understanding human beings in their contexts and then responding in partnership with others. Our efforts have a greater chance for effectiveness when we have guidelines to follow. Theory and model-building efforts provide these guidelines. In taking on this work, not only do social workers incorporate the values I already mentioned, but we also understand that our theories and models are incomplete, subject to modification as we identity new information.

Theory and model-building in social work requires the on-going testing of our assumptions, theories, and models and how and whether we are implementing our shared values. Social workers who are effective change their assumptions, theories, and models when new evidence arises.

A document whose formatting does not fit for this collection is "A Logic Model for Model Building in Social Work." This document is available at http://www.scribd.com/doc/110832777/A-Logic-Model-for-Model-Building-in-Social-Work. Each of the documents in this book is available separately on scribd.com & many on Amazon.

Jane Gilgun
December 20, 2012
Minneapolis, Minnesota, USA

CONTENTS

University of Minnesota, Twin Cities, USA
School of Social Work
SW 8861 Theory & Model Building in Social Work
Fall 2012
Jane F. Gilgun, PhD, LICSW

Course Syllabus

This is a PhD-level course that prepares students to analyze, develop, test, and modify theories and models relevant to social work practice. The course is practical and applied and requires that students learn by doing; that is, they work with theories and models that are in use today. By doing this, students will build their skills for analyzing, modifying, and developing models and theories.

In this course, social work practice is defined as activities that social workers carry out in various contexts, such as work in policy, community organization, social development, organizational development and management, direct practice, and any other domains where social workers have a presence. The methods for working with theories and models that we examine in this course are responsive to these multiple domains.

Models, in general, are representations of how things work. Social workers continually test models in that we compare the models we develop to how things actually work in particular situations. We change our models in response to what we notice in particular situations. To widen the scope of what we notice, the notion of negative cases is important. We search for aspects of situations that do not fit our models and therefore do not fit our expectations. We want to identify and include the exceptions so that our models are as inclusive as possible. Since we continuously apply models to new situations and since new situations typically contain aspects of situations that our models do not anticipate, our models are subject to on-going modifications.

In social work, models often include representations of what happens when we perform actions. Social work interventions are examples of action models. Action models or models of interventions represent processes that have contexts, antecedents, experiences, interpretations, and consequences. Model developers also are prepared for unanticipated consequences and have developed procedures to respond to them.

Theories underlie models. Theories, in general, are representations of relationships among concepts. Theories may describe, categorize, or explain, or do a combination of these. Descriptions of multi-faceted social issues that are organized through concepts are the basis of higher order theorizing and can provide a foundation for model-building.

An example of how theories are part of models is the following. In order to develop a model that represents procedures for intervening into issues related to poverty, model developers must have an idea of what poverty is. Often model developers have relatively unarticulated theory that is part of broader perspectives upon which models are based. These broader perspectives contain not only relatively undefined theories but also amalgams of ideologies, biases, values of various sorts, professional and personal experiences, and, hopefully, research. A key question in this course is where theory comes from. Another is whether and how theory informs models.

Involvement of community practitioners, policy makers, and service users appears to be a most promising route to the development of useful and effective theories and models. The course will emphasize the teamwork involved in theory and model development.

Theories and models that are consistent with the values and mission of social work have explicit or implicit values such as justice, care, respect for autonomy, and dignity and worth of the person, start where clients are (understand as well as possible how service users experience their worlds), and view the focus

2

of their practice as persons in interaction with various environments.

Theories and models can be at various levels of abstraction and can account for sequences of processes, such a model of participatory action research with low-income women on Sullivan Island, South Carolina, or for parts of a process, such as a model of assessing children with cerebral palsy and their families.

Important questions are where theories and models come from. The course will introduce two or more methods of theory development that can be linked to models of practice. Students will gain expertise in these methods of theory development over the course of their studies in other courses and in their subsequent research experience. This course represents only a beginning, a handshake.

Course Goals & Objectives

The overall goals of the course are to develop students' understandings of the characteristics of social work theories and models of practice, to help them to develop a framework to analyze theories and models of practice, and to help them to begin the process of acquiring skills in theory and model building.

By the end of the course, students will have a growing sense of

- tensions between logical-rational models of practice and human sciences models;
- their own philosophies of science and when logical-rational models apply and when human sciences models apply;
- how social work thought and values connect to human sciences traditions such as starting where clients are, person-environment interactions, and social justice/care values;

- how to integrate their personal and professional values and experiences into the theories and models of practice that they develop;
- how issues related to power, gender, ethnicity, age, sexual identity, ability, social class, physical & personality characteristics, income, and other indicators of social "worth" and location can be built into theories and into models of practice;
- growing expertise in integrating various sources of information and ideas into modifying existing theories and models of practice and creating their own theories and models of practice;
- how some models of practice contribute to assessment, some to intervention, some to evaluation, and some that encompass these three areas of practice; and
- that models of practice can be created to respond to issues related to policy, community organization, social development, organizational development and management, direct practice, and any other domains of social work practice.

The course will build on students' own experiences and interests and will show them that the ideas that are embedded in these goals and objectives are already part of how they view the world. In many ways, this course will help students give names to and to contextualize how they already think about theory and model building as well as advance their knowledge of this field.

The course is responsive to the statement of the Group for the Advancement of Social Work Education (GADE) on doctoral education.

The conception of doctoral education as creating "stewards of the discipline" (Carnegie Foundation, 2002) means preparing students for the tasks of generation, conservation, and transformation of knowledge (Anastas et al, 2003, Guidelines for Quality in Social Work Doctoral Programs (Revised), pp. 7-8).

Course Expectations for Students

1. Students are expected to attend all class sessions and to participate in class activities and discussion. Definitions of class participation appear later in this syllabus. Students are expected to notify the professor--in advance, whenever possible-- regarding absences, including unavoidable reasons to leave class early. Persistent absence, lateness to class, and lateness in submitting papers will be considered in assigning final grades.

Please keep in mind that coming to class late is disruptive to other students and to the professor and can detract from the quality of the class experience. Also, though eating in class may be necessary for health reasons, please refrain from eating food that crackles, crunches, and snaps or whose packaging crackles, crunches, and snaps or otherwise makes noises that are distracting.

Missing four or more classes will result in failure of the course except for documented medical circumstances. For students who miss class for medical reasons, the missed work will have to be made up.

2. Students are expected to complete all assigned readings and written assignments prior to the class for which they has been assigned and are expected to be able to integrate that reading into class discussions and activities.

3. Students are expected to make use of University libraries and resources for assignments for research purposes;

4. Students will be expected to have access to the Internet and to use resources on the World Wide Web as directed in this course;

5. All assignments are to be typed, written in non-sexist language, and follow the format of the American Psychological Association Publication Manual (6th ed.). Papers should be turned in with no errors in spelling, punctuation, or grammar. Papers will not be accepted after the due date without an acceptable reason for a late paper.

6. Students give proper credit to originators of ideas that they use in their written work and in oral presentations. They also must not use the work of others without attributions. Both are forms of piracy and violate the policies of the School of Social

Work and the University Student Conduct Code. The Council of Science Editors (2009) gives the following definition of piracy.

> Piracy is defined as the appropriation of ideas, data, or methods from others without adequate permission or acknowledgment. Again, deceit plays a central role in this form of misconduct. The intent of the perpetrator is the untruthful portrayal of the ideas or methods as his or her own.

> Plagiarism is a form of piracy that involves the use of text or other items (figures, images, tables) without permission or acknowledgment of the source of these materials. Plagiarism generally involves the use of materials from others, but can apply to researchers' duplication of their own previously published reports without acknowledgment (this is sometimes called self-plagiarism or duplicate publication).

Students who attach their names to the writings and ideas of others without attribution to the actual author(s), whether the writings and ideas are published or unpublished, are subject to charges of academic misconduct and may be suspended or expelled from the University of Minnesota. Piracy is theft of intellectual property that places appearances above integrity.

7. Students are expected to offer the professor clear, constructive feedback regarding course content and teaching methods. Students are expected to complete confidential evaluations of the course using the University's standardized form at the end of the semester.

8. Students may not use an assignment completed in another course for the present course. This includes papers, answer to a test question, or any other material used for a grade in another class. If students do so, they will not be given credit for the assignment; and

9. Incompletes are given only in extraordinary circumstances. The School of Social Work's policy on incompletes requires the student to develop a contract with the professor that will describe the work which remains to be completed and the date by which the work must be submitted to the professor. In

addition to providing the professor with a copy of the complete contract on incompletes, the student must file a copy of the contract with the director of graduate students at the School of Social Work. The policy states that incomplete course grades will be converted to an F grade if not completed within two semesters.

When students use material from their practice, please remember that as professionals, we have ethical responsibilities to maintain client confidentiality. The professor will disguise the identities of clients and expects students to abide by this ethical value.

Course Expectations for the Professor

1. The professor will use a variety of instructional methods including short lectures, case studies to illustrate points of the lectures, the use of electronic slides, large and small group discussions and exercises, and individual activities to address varieties of learning styles.
2. The professor will provide a clear structure for the course and each class session through the syllabus, statements of purpose of each class, guiding discussion, providing appropriate linkages between topics, and summarizing main points throughout the semester.
3. Student assignments will include clear expectations and, where possible, opportunities for student selection of alternatives. Barring exceptional circumstances, student assignments will be returned within one week of submission.
4. The professor will be available on issues related to class assignments or content during office hours, by phone, e-mail, or by appointment.
5. The professor will work to facilitate an atmosphere in the classroom that is conducive to learning, is non-threatening, and is respectful of a variety of learning styles.
6. When students work together in groups, the professor will be available for consultation and to assist groups in completing their tasks.

7. The professor will provide feedback to students that identifies strengths and areas for improvement in a constructive manner.

Plan of the Course

The course meets three hours per week on Tuesdays during the fall semester. There will be one 15-minute break half-way through the class. Class sessions include lectures, large and small group discussions, small group work, and student presentations. During these activities, students are strongly encouraged to apply course learnings to their work with individuals, families, groups, communities, legislative bodies, and any other areas where they have practiced.

Readings

There are no required texts, but there are required and optional articles. Additional readings will be assigned over the course of the semester. Students will be responsible for developing a reading list that is relevant to their interests.

The journal articles are available through University libraries e-journals.

You must do the readings and complete class assignments every week in order to understand and contribute to class discussions and other activities, as well as to foster your own learning. Class activities are based on the assumption that students have done the readings and any other tasks the professor may assign. As you read for this course, you will come upon many terms that you may not understand, such as "the Hawthorne effect" and "maturation" in various types of experiments. It is your responsibility to find definitions of these terms and think of how they may apply to the development, implementation, and evaluation of models of practice.

You are required to use a minimum of five articles and chapters assigned in this course in your midterm and 10 articles and chapters assigned in the course for the final paper/project.

Besides the required readings, students are to use a minimum of three more articles, books, and book chapters than those required for the midterm and five more for the final. When students work with others on midterm and final projects, their products will have more references and more elaboration than products on which students work alone.

Some students may have little background in theory and model development. In these situations, I recommend the following texts, journals, and articles. While many of them do not directly discuss theory and model building, they have the components of theory and modeling-building that are the focus of this course.

Altschuld, James W. & Belle Ruth Witkin (2000). *From needs assessment to action: Transforming needs into solution strategies.* Thousand Oaks, CA: Sage.

Jacard, James & Jacob Jacoby (2010). *Theory construction and model-building skills: A practical guide for social scientists.* New York: Guilford.

Mertens, Donna M. (2009). *Transformative research and evaluation.* New York: Guilford.

King, Joyce E. (Ed.). (2005). *Black education: A transformative research and action agenda for the new century.* New York: Routledge.

Lewin, Kurt (1946). Action research and minority problems. *Journal of Social Issues 2(4)*, 34-46,

Reason, Peter & Bradbury, Hillary (Eds.) (2006). *Handbook of action research.* Thousand Oaks, CA: Sage

Reflective Practice. This is a journal with articles that show how reflective practices contribute to models of practice.

Research on Social Work Practice. The January 2010 issue of this journal has several articles on intervention research.

Rothman, Jack & Edwin Thomas (Eds). (1994). *Intervention research: Design and development for human services.* Binghamton, N.Y: Haworth.

Saleebey, Dennis (2008). *The strengths perspective in social work practice* (5th ed.). Boston: Allyn & Bacon.

Schön, Donald A. (1983). *The reflective practitioner: How professionals think in action.* New York: Basic.

Van de Ven, Andrew H. (2007). *Engaged scholarship: A guide for organizational and social research.* New York: Oxford.

The requirements are as follows.

- reading the weekly assignments and sharing your observations in class discussions;
- completing periodic written assignments and posting them to the course's Google group located at https://groups.google.com/forum/#!forum/theory-and-model-building-in-social-work
- commenting on a minimum of two postings of colleagues on Google groups each time a posting occurs;
- an interview;
- lead class discussions of readings;
- a midterm project;
- a final project.

The following is a description of the assignments.

1. **An interview** with a social work researcher, program developer, or direct practitioner about either 1) how they develop models of practice/interventions that are used on a agency-wide basis or 2) the place of professional experience, research, theory, values, and service user perspectives in the models of practice that they use. For either topic, ask the person you interview a series of questions:

- describe the model of practice;
- whether and when they developed logic models;
- what they think of evidence-based practice;
- whether there is paperwork involved in implementing this model;
- If there is paperwork, how do service providers feel about the paperwork;
- any provisions for modifying how service users implement the model;
- the place of fidelity to treatment protocols in the

implementation of the model; if yes, how?

Also, discuss whether the people you interview were more concerned that the model was useful to service users or whether they were more concerned with whether they applied theory accurately. There may be other questions and topics of interest to you and the interviewee. Please feel free to address them.

You may videotape this interview if you wish and if the interviewee is amenable. You can show excerpts of the interview in class. Otherwise you will do a brief oral report in class and turn in a 3-5 page account of the interview the following week. The professor will provide further details in class. Due any time up until class 13, November 27. 10 points.

2. **One brief article** that you write for the general public and that you post on scribd.com, wordpress, or other social publishing website. Between 500 to 1000 words. Due any time up to class 13, November 27. 10 points.

3. **Midterm assignment.** 25 points. The midterm assignment is a reflective piece. In this assignment, you will discuss your personal and professional values and the relevance of these values to your practice of social work, the practice of social work in general, and in theory and model building. In addition, I would like you to reflect upon by yourself and with others the values that service users/target populations might have. While this is a reflective piece, I also want you to consult other social workers through one or more interviews and through reading to get their perspectives on the roles of values in relation to these topics. The NASW Code of Ethics is a place to start, but I also want you to do some searches for references on values and practice, including the practice of theory and model building/intervention research. Length: up to 12 pages for single-authored papers and 18 pages for multiple-authored papers. Due Class 8, October 23.

4. **Final project**, 40 points. This final project is your opportunity to show that you can apply course learnings to theory and model building. In this assignment, you can

- analyze an existing model of practice and/or theory relevant to social work;
- modify an existing model of practice or theory;
- create a new model of practice or put together a new theory of practice for a particular domain and show how you will test the model or theory.

The theories and models of practice that you work with in this assignment are likely to be "partial," meaning they focus on a particular aspect of practice, such as assessment, intervention, or evaluation, or involve testing a particular model of practice through task analysis, or involve an informed analysis of a method of theory-testing/theory-building. Length: up to 14 pages for sole authored papers and up to 20 pages for multiple-authored papers. Due Monday, December 17 at midnight.

Students may negotiate with the professor another kind of final project. Students will present drafts of these final papers during the last two classes of the semester, which are classes 14 and 15, December 4 and 11.

5. **Class participation**. 15 points. Class participation includes contributions that students' writing assignments make to the course. These assignments will be discussed in class and will also have written instructions. Contributions that add to the learning environment are particularly valuable.

This is an interactive course, with students involved not only in small group discussions, but also in presenting weekly or biweekly written assignments related to that day's topic. Further descriptions of definitions of class participation are in the first two items of "course expectations for students," above and in a few paragraphs later in this syllabus. Students may perform additional tasks throughout the semester as the professor and students see opportunities arise.

Grading

Interview	10 points
Brief article	10 points
Midterm project	15 points
Final project	40 points
Class participation	15 points

The criteria for evaluating these assignments are generally those of any graduate-level course. Papers will be graded on critical thinking, organization, and ability to write clearly. Critical thinking includes supporting ideas with evidence, being even-handed in representing the views of others, evaluating the ideas of others according to explicit criteria, providing alternatives to ideas students find are suboptimal, and demonstrations of abilities to synthesize, critique, and apply course learnings.

Organization generally means the work has a logical flow from one main point to the next and that each paragraph begins with a topic sentence followed by elaboration of the point the topic sentence makes. APA style requires the use of headings, and headings help demonstrate the logical flow — or organization — of papers and other assignments. Be sure to develop an introduction and a concluding discussion for the papers and course projects.

Additional markers of excellence include supporting and illustrating general ideas with examples, abilities to apply social work principles, ethics, and empathy to course work, and the ability to show clients' points of view; e.g., to bring client perspectives to life.

In addition to having a well-thought out paper with the above characteristics, each paper must have a title page, an introduction, a concluding discussion section, and, of course, a well-designed main body.

If students are unclear about or dissatisfied with grading, conversations about grading standards and expectations are welcome.

Besides engaging actively in the activities discussed above, in general, class participation means students' active engagement in class discussion and activities in ways that enhance class discussion. In their comments, students demonstrate their understanding of the many ideas--and their applications--important to theory and modeling building in social work. Class participation is a strong indicator that students do the assigned reading every week, complete written assignments conscientiously, and are thinking about the implications of the readings for practice. Respect for and openness to the points of view of others are important dimensions of class participation.

Please do not interrupt others, speak without regard for others who might want to speak, and monopolize class time. Your professor will talk to students who demonstrate these behaviors. Resistance to changing these behaviors will be reflected in the course grade for class participation. Sometimes students are so enthusiastic about course content that they monopolize class time. In these cases, your professor will gently ask them to save some of their comments for discussion with the professor after class, over the internet, or during office hours. Lateness to class and missing class also affects quality of students' participation and are considered in the assignment of points for class participation.

For this course, the grade of A denotes superior performance that is both consistent and outstanding. A's are given when the point range is between 93 and 100. A-'s are given when the point range is between 92 and 90. The grade of B denotes good, steady adequate performance, with some of the plus values that make for an A. B+'s are given when the point range is between 89 and 88. B's are given when the points are between 87 and 83. B-'s are given when the points range from 82 to 80.

The B student shows understanding and ability to integrate learning and ends the course with a comprehensive grasp of the material. The grade of C denotes a performance that is barely acceptable and is probably adequate to complete the next course in a sequence. C+'s are given when the point range is between 78 and 79. C's are given when the points range between 77 and 73. C-'s, are for grades between 72 and 70. The grade of D denotes unacceptable work and some comprehension of course material and no probability of being able to complete the next course in a sequence. The grade of D is given when the point range is between 60 and 69. The grade of F denotes failure--that is, unacceptable performance: an inability to understand the material. F's are given when the total points are 50 or below. P denotes a grade of A to C+.

Policy on the Use of Student Papers

At times, the professor may ask students for a copy of their papers to use as a sample paper for students in future classes. If asked, students have the right to refuse without fear of reprisals, and your professor will ask students to sign a form indicating that they have freely given the professor's permission to use their paper as a sample paper.

Supportive Learning Environments

The development of a supportive learning environment is fundamental to this course. Learning takes place in the free exchange of ideas. In such a course, listening to and appreciating the points of view of others, eliciting ideas from others, and articulating your own points of view will foster a supportive learning environment. As discussed in relation to class participation, some enthusiastic students may talk to the point where others feel they are monopolizing class time. Please monitor yourself and be open if others suggest you may be monopolizing.

Please turn off all cell phones and pagers during class time. Do not surf the web or check e-mail during class. If I see you doing any of this, I will ask you to stop immediately.

We all have been exposed to sexist, racist, homophobic, classist, and ableist ideas and practices. We cannot be blamed for misinformation we have absorbed, but we will be held responsible for being open to alternative points of view. In addition, we will be held accountable for repeating misinformation once we have learned otherwise. We each have obligations to combat the myths and stereotypes about our own groups and other groups so that we can turn walls into bridges and thus promote the common welfare. As we will discuss in class, these values are deeply embedded in the NASW Code of Ethics and the Code of Ethics of the International Federation of Social Workers.

Please do not use scented personal care products when in Peters Hall. Several persons who are part of the School of Social Work community become ill, and sometimes their reactions could be life-threatening, when exposed to a wide variety of scents. I will ask persons who wear scented products in classrooms or other enclosed areas to leave if there are persons with chemical sensitivities in that area. Persons with environmental illnesses greatly appreciate your efforts.

The professor will provide reasonable accommodations to persons with disabilities to give them an equal opportunity to achieve success in their graduate education. Students seeking accommodations must work with the University of Minnesota's Office of Disability Services. This office determines eligibility and makes recommendations for reasonable accommodations. This office can be reached at 612/624-8281.

This syllabus is subject to revision over the course of the semester when there is reason to do so. This is in the spirit of the scientific method.

CLASS SCHEDULE AND READINGS

Class 1
Introductions
Overview of the Course
Theory & Model Building in Social Work

Class 2
Theories & Models
Variety in Theories & Models
Components of Theories & Models

Readings

Gilgun, Jane F. (2011). Theory and case study research. Smashwords.

Ropella, Glen G, C. Anthony Hunt, & Dev A. Nagi (2005). Using heuristic models to bridge the gap between analytic and experimental models in biology. Paper presented at the 2005 Spring Simulation Multiconference, April 2-8, San Diego, CA.

Answer the following questions about the above readings. Please be brief—a full page more or less, double spaced, for answers to the questions.

1. Can we construct theories from a single case? Discuss the arguments for and against this practice. Use examples.
2. How did Ropella et al describe what a model is?
3. What do you think of their description?
4. What are the similarities between biology and social work? What are the differences?
5. Write down two take-away ideas from each article and be prepared to share them in class.

Examples of Models Using Theory

Gilgun, Jane F. (2010). *The NEATS: A Child & Family Assessment.* Available from the professor.

Rolland, J.S. (2005). Cancer and the family: An integrative model. *Cancer,* 104(11sup), 2584-2595.

Answer the following questions regarding the examples. Make each answer brief, a page or less double spaced.

1. What are the sources of the authors' theories and models that are in each article?

2. Is the writing of these two pieces understandable to their intended audiences? First, note who the intended audiences are. Be sure to state what you think is important when communicating with these audiences. Give examples of the points that you make.

Class 3
Intervention Research

Readings

Abell, Neil & David Wolf. (2003). Implementing intervention research in doctoral education. *Journal of Teaching in Social Work, 23(1),* 3-19.
Fraser, Mark W., & Maeda J. Galinsky (2010). Steps in intervention research: Designing and developing social programs. *Research on Social Work Practice, 20,* 459-466.

Examples

Comer, Edna, Andrea Meier, & Maeda J. Galinksky (2003). Development of innovative group work practice using the intervention research paradigm. *Social Work, 49(2),* 250-260.

Answer the following questions.

1. What are the sources of information that go into the construction of the models of practice/the construction of interventions that are discussed in the readings?
2. What roles do theory play?
3. Is there anything you would have liked to have seen in these articles that are not there?
4. What do you think of intervention research so far?
5. Is intervention research something you've done or would like to do?
6. Write a question that you would like to answer and then answer it.

Task

Explore the Campbell Collaboration with particular attention to topics that are of interest to you. Jot down a few notes about your responses and be prepared to share them in class. Take special notice about whether the reviews examine how the interventions they are evaluating have been constructed.

Class 4
Intervention Research

Readings

Gilgun, Jane F. & Roberta G. Sands (2012). The contributions of qualitative approaches to developmental intervention research. *Research on Social Work Practice, 11(4)*, 349-361.

Rothman, Jack (1991). A model of case management: Toward am empirically based practice. *Social Work, 36(6)*, 520-528.

Read one of the "classic" articles on intervention research that are in the reference list of either of these articles. The classic authors are Thomas, Rothman, and Reid.

Example

Block, Ellen (2012). "That's what I see:' Enhancing AIDS intervention research through deep ethnography. *Research on Social Work Practice, 11(4)*, 379-394.

Mokuau, Noreen et al (2008). Development of a family intervention for native Hawaiian women with cancer: A pilot study. *Social Work, 53(1)*, 9-19.

Answer the following questions.

1. What are the sources of information that go into the construction of the models of practice/the construction of interventions?
2. What roles do theory play?
3. Is there anything you would have liked to have seen in these articles that are not there?
4. What do you think of intervention research so far?
5. Is this something you've done or would like to do?
6. Can you identify any implicit or explicit values in any of these articles.
6. Write a question that you would like to answer and then answer it.

Class 5
Evidence-Based Practice

Readings

APA Taskforce on Evidence-Based Practice (2006). Evidence-based practice in psychology. *American Psychologist, 61(4)*, 271-185.

Blow, Adrian J., Douglas H. Sprenkle, & Sean D. Davis (2007). Is who delivers the treatment more important than the treatment itself? The role of the therapist in common factors. *Journal of Marital and Family Therapy, 33(3)*, 298-317.

Gambrill, Eileen (2001). Social work: An authority-based profession. *Research on Social Work Practice, 11(2)*, 166-175.

Tannenbaum, Sandra J. (2004). Evidence-based practice as mental health policy: Three controversies and a caveat. *Health Affairs, 24(1)*, 163-173.

Written assignment on separate sheet

Class 6
Evidence-Based Practice

Readings

Gilgun, Jane F. (2010, November). The nature of practice in evidence-based practice. Paper presented at the Theory Construction and Research Methodology Pre-Conference Workshop, National Council on Family Relations, Minneapolis, Minnesota, November 3.

Gilgun, Jane F. (2005). The four cornerstones of evidence-based practice in social work. *Research on Social Work Practice*, 15(1), 52-61.

Gray, Mel & Leanne Schubert (2010) Turning base metal into gold: Transmuting art, practice, research, and experience into gold. *British Journal of Social Work, 40*, 2308-2325.

Murdach, Allison (2010). What good is soft evidence? *Social Work, 55(4)*, 309-316.

Written assignment on separate sheet

Class 7
Common Factor Models of Psychotherapy Research with Applications to Social Work

Readings

Blow, Adrian J., Douglas H. Sprenkle, & Sean D. Davis (2007). Is who delivers the treatment more important than the treatment itself? The role of the therapist in common factors. *Journal of Marital and Family Therapy, 33(3)*, 298-317.

Cameron, Mark, & Elizabeth King Keenan (2010). The common factors model: Implications for transtheoretical clinical social work practice. *Social Work, 55(1)*, 63-73.

Drisko, James W. (2004). Common factors in psychotherapy outcome. *Families in Society, 85 (1)*, 81-90.

Lambert, M. (1992). Implications of outcome research for psychotherapy integration. In J. Norcross & J. Goldstein (Eds.), *Handbook of psychotherapy integration* (pp. 94-129) NY: Basic.

Written assignment on separate sheet

Class 8
Logic Models
Reflections on & Integration of Course Learning
Applications of Course Learnings

Readings

Alter, Catherine & Marcia Egan. (1997). Logic modeling: A tool for teaching critical thinking in social work practice. *Journal of Social Work Education, 33(1)*, 85-102.   Kaplan, Sue A. & Catherine E. Garrett (2005). The use of logic models for community-based initiatives. *Evaluation and program planning, 28*, 167-172.

W.K. Kellogg Foundation (2004). Logic model development guide: Using logic models to bring together planning, evaluation, and action.
http://ww2.wkkf.org/DesktopModules/WKF.00_DmaSupport/ViewDoc.aspx?fld=PDFFile&CID=281&ListID=28&ItemID=2813669&LanguageID=0

No written assignment
No interviews

****Mid-Term Papers Due***

Class 9
More on Logic Models
Theory Development

Readings

Gilgun, Jane F. (2008, April). Deductive qualitative analysis as middle ground, paper presented at the Midwest Conference on Qualitative Research, St. Paul, MN, USA, April 18.

Hunter, David E. K. (2006). Using a theory of change approach to build organization strength, capacity and sustainability with not-for-profit organizations in the human services section. *Evaluation and Program Planning, 29*, 193-200.

Maxwell, Joseph (2004). Using qualitative methods for causal explanation. *Field Methods, 16*, 243-264.

Renger, Ralph & Carolyn Hurley (2006). From theory to practice: Lessons learned in the application of the ATM approach to developing logic models. *Evaluation and Program Planning (29)*, 106–119.

Written assignment on separate sheet

Class 10
Theory Development
Consequences of Incomplete Models

Readings

Gilgun, Jane F. (2010). Philosophy of science and mental health research: Where are studies of effects of MI on families? *Current Issues in Qualitative Research, 1(8)*, 1-4. http://www.scribd.com/doc/36464225/Philosophies-of-Science-Mental-Health-Research-Where-are-Studies-of-Effects-of-MI-on-Families

Gilgun, Jane F. (2010). The intellectual roots of ground theory. *Report, quarterly magazine of the National Council on Family Relations, 55 (2)*, 5-8. Available at http://www.scribd.com/doc/43142136/The-Intellectual-Roots-of-Grounded-Theory

Gilgun, Jane F. (2005). Qualitative research and family psychology. *Journal of Family Psychology,19(1)*, 40-50.

Written assignment on separate sheet

Class 11
Theory Development
Reflections on & Integration of Course Learnings
Applications of Course Learnings

Readings

Gilgun, Jane F. (2003). Preliminary studies, hypothesis testing, and qualitative research. Unpublished manuscript. St. Paul, MN: School of Social Work, University of Minnesota.

Gilgun, Jane F. (2007, November). The legacy of the Chicago School of Sociology for Family Theory Building. Paper presented at the Preconference Workshop on Theory Construction and Research Methodology, National Council on Family Relations, Pittsburgh, PA, USA, November 7.

Greenberg, Leslie & Florence Foerster (1996). Task analysis exemplified: The process of resolving unfinished business. *Journal of Consulting and Clinical Psychology, 64(3)*, 439-446.

Written assignment on separate sheet

Class 12
Theory & Model Development
Integration of Course Learnings

Readings & Assignment

To be announced

Class 13
Theory Development
Task Analysis as Model Testing
A Framework for Analysis

Readings

Berlin, Sharon B., Katherine B. Mann, & Susan F. Grossman, (1991). Task analysis of cognitive therapy for depression. *Social Work Research & Abstracts, 27 (2)*, 3-11.

Gilgun, Jane F. (in press). Grounded theory, deductive qualitative analysis, and social work research and practice. *Qualitative Methods in Social Work* (2nd ed.), William Reid & Anne E. Fortune (Eds.). New York: Columbia University Press.

Assignment

Find an article relevant to your topic for the final project and that uses theory to guide the development of the intervention and or theory that could be applied to interventions.

Written assignment on separate sheet

Class 14
Dissemination
A Framework for Analysis
Student Presentations

Readings
Gilgun, Jane F. (2005). "Grab" and good science: Writing up the results of qualitative research. *Qualitative Health Research*, 15(2), 256-262.

Friese, Bettina & Karen Bogenschneider (2009). The voice of experience: How social scientists communicate family research to policy makers. *Family Relations, 58*, 229-243.

Ling, Jack C., Barbara A.K. Franklin, Janis F. Lindsteadt, & Susan A.N. Gearon (1992). Social marketing: Its place in public health. *Review of Public Health (13)*, 341-362).

Review governmental websites, NGO websites, social publishing websites, YouTube, and your favorite scholarly journal, among others, to see the variety of web-based dissemination models.

Class 15
Summary: Theory & Model-Building in Social Work
Student Presentations

Projects due Monday, December 17 at midnight

ESSAY

Evidence, Even-Handedness, & Transparency in Critical Thinking

By Jane Gilgun

Summary

This article describes some of the characteristics of critical thinking. The main point is that description comes before analysis. In order to analyze or criticize anything, we first have to describe whatever it is that we are analyzing/criticizing and do so in an even-handed way. Critical thinking is a respectful way of understanding the points of view of others and putting forth our own points of view. Critical thinking can be complex. Values of fairness and justice support the principles of critical thinking. This article sets out some of the basic principles.

Evidence, Even-Handedness, & Transparency in Critical Thinking

After years of university-based research and teaching, I have developed an appreciation of the principles of critical thinking. Individuals who do good work follow these principles. By good work, I mean developing an understanding of the topics that are relevant to their work and being aware of the implications and consequences of their work for persons who are in these situations. Those who do good work operate on the most basic of ethical principles: Do no harm. Other values that support critical thinking include fairness and justice.

Evidence

Critical thinking involves understanding the points of views and experiences of others as well as understanding one's own. To do this, individuals take the time to understand others and their situations. They listen to persons who will be affected by their work. They seek to understand the perspectives, experiences, values, and wants of these persons. When they read research reports and other sources of information, they seek to understand what the authors are saying in the authors' own terms. They appreciate the time, often years, it takes authors to formulate their ideas and then to write them down.

Individuals who are competent critical thinkers do not move immediately to judgment, criticism, and questioning. They take the time and make the effort to be sure they understand whatever it is they ultimately will make decisions about. It helps to talk to others or to write down what they believe the issues are and then discuss their understanding of the issues with others, including persons their decisions affect.

Competent critical thinkers reflect upon their own experiences, seek out their own possible biases, attempt not to distort their understandings of the perspectives of others because of their biases, and use their personal experiences in ways that increases their understandings of the situations of others. At the same time, they understand that their personal experiences may not fit the experiences of others. They seek and celebrate individual differences, as long as differences do no harm.

They also reflect upon their own values and the values of others. They are honest with themselves if their values limit their appreciation of the values of others, when the values of others do no harm. They evaluate their own values in terms of whether or not their values do harm.

In summary, good critical thinkers seek multiple sources of information and reflect upon their own experiences and values in order to develop experiential understandings (empathy) of the situations of others. They also are reflective in order to raise their awareness of their own biases so as to avoid allowing their biases to distort understandings of various types of information. They think through the possible consequences of any actions they make take on the basis of their understandings. They describe before they analyze, questions, and criticize.

Information becomes evidence when it is used as the basis of judgments and actions.

Even-Handedness

What's especially important in gathering information is to seek out persons and sources that are likely to have perspectives that are different from our own. Critical thinkers are even handed. Their understandings are even-handed. When they discuss the issues with others, they are even-handed. When they write about the issues, they are even-handed. That means they represent the points of view of others fairly and without distortion, even when they don't agree with some of the points of view of others.

Transparency

When individuals have taken into account multiple points of view, they are positioned to evaluate the information and formulate plans of action. The key word in evaluating information and taking actions is transparency. Transparency includes definition of terms, comprehensive descriptions of the issues, evaluation of the information, and consideration of consequences.

Definitions of Terms

Most terms have many different meanings. In order to have a cogent and compelling evaluation of information, critical thinkers discuss the various meanings of key terms. They then define the terms as they use them in their own work. In addition, similar concepts may have different names. It's important to review the various terms that cover similar concepts and state the term or terms that they use. Often individuals give reasons for their choices of terms.

For example, if the task is to evaluate information about theory and model building in social work, the first step is to review the various definitions of "theory" and of "model building" and then define those terms for the purposes of your analysis of the information.

Description

The next step is to present the even-handed comprehensive information you have gathered about your topic. If your topic is violence against women, then you present descriptive material about violence against women. This involves presenting descriptive material that that creates a comprehensive picture of the issues. You do not have to present every issue that is relevant. Typically, what is covered is the scope of the issue, the factors that contribute to the issue, the meanings of the issue to the people involved, the consequences of the issue, and how social policy, prevention, and intervention issues have addressed the issue.

Principled Evaluations

Once critical thinkers have presented a solid description of the issue, then they evaluate the issue. The meaning of the word "evaluate" includes transparency and careful appraisal. They state the principles they have applied in the evaluation.

For example, in the evaluation of information about violence against women in families, a possible evaluative principle is whether in descriptions of outcomes of the violence, there also are descriptions of factors that are associated with women recovering from violence or coping adequately with its effects. Critical thinkers would state how these factors could contribute to policies, programs, and interventions and how they may be characteristic of naturally occurring resilience.

A generally acceptable definition of resilience is coping with, adapting to, and overcoming adversities. In addition to providing a working definition of resilience, a critical thinker would also list qualities associated with resilience, such as capacities for secure attachment to others where individuals can process the meanings of the violence, identify other prosocial coping capacities, and maintain emotional availability to children if there are children in the families where violence has occurred.

The point here is that when critical thinkers want to evaluate information that they have presented in even-handed ways, they have to be clear (transparent) about the principles/ideas/research on which they base their evaluation.

There may be biases related to gender in available evidence on violence against women, or a bias against certain kinds of research in a presentation of research on a particular intervention, such as social planning. An analysis based on the principles of critical thinking would state that such bias exists, present evidence of a bias, and show why the bias may be harmful and to whom. Then an analysis based on critical thinking would make suggestion about how to redress the bias.

Strategies for Deeper Understanding

It is helpful to review published reviews of topics that are of interest to persons wanting to develop their skills in critical thinking. These reviews will show critical thinking at work without stating that the authors are following the principles of critical thinking. The internet is a trove of information about principles of critical thinking. Do a bit of reading about critical thinking on the internet and then find review articles on topics of your choice and see how these articles apply or do not apply principles of critical thinking.

Summary:
Description Comes Before Analysis

Description comes before analysis. In order to analyze anything, we first have to describe whatever it is that we are analyzing and do so in an even-handed way. This can take time and thought. Rarely or not at all do scholars understand complex social issues without a lot of thought.

In addition, analysis is based upon principles that we explain. Analysis is a transparent process where we show audiences the bases of our analyses. Descriptions and analysis require reflection upon what we think and the values behind what we think. We are honest about our own biases and anything else that might get in the way of even-handedness.

Critical thinking is a respectful way of understanding the points of view of others and putting forth our own points of view. Through critical thinking we develop an even-handed understanding of persons in their situations. We thus position ourselves to make recommendations that may be helpful in terms of policies, practice, and prevention.

University of Minnesota, Twin Cities
School of Social Work
SW 8361 Theory & Model Building
in Social Work
Fall 2012
Jane F. Gilgun, Ph.D., LICSW

Checklist for Assessments of Definitions

____The definition explains the meanings of the term.

____ The definitions shows more than one dimension of the meaning of the term.

____ The definition draws on two or more sources. [For today's class, this means more than one reading.]

____The definition shows that there can be more than one meaning attached to the term.

____ The definition does not include the term that is being defined.

____ The definition shows what the term means and does not mean.

____ The definition is written in every day language.

____ The definition is both conceptual and operational. [This means that the definition includes a general statement about what the word means and then provides one or more examples of the general statement.]

____ The definition is a work in progress, or a working definition. [A working definition is one that users know do not contain all that everyone else says is part of the meaning of the term. It is a definition that users believe is useful for their purposes and that they will add to as they work on their projects.]

__Note:__ This exercise is to formalize bits and pieces of what it means to be a critical thinker. A critical thinker has at the minimum a working definition of terms. Working definitions mean that the users understand that their definitions are incomplete and require further delineation.

University of Minnesota, Twin Cities, USA
School of Social Work
SW 8861 Theory & Model Building
in Social Work
Fall 2012

What is Developmental
Intervention Research?

Jane F. Gilgun

What is intervention research? In England the term means *evaluation research*. To be respectful of what others think intervention research is, the term *developmental intervention research* might work better. *Developmental* as a term has a history. Thomas (1978) first called "intervention research" "developmental research." It's also consistent with the work of program evaluators like Patton (2011) who said that programs are never fixed but undergo continual development.

Practitioners, including researchers, learn something new as they evaluate programs. Patton's focus is on program development through evaluation, but his thought can be applied to the development, testing, and modification of interventions, which is the scope of developmental intervention research. As will be shown later, developmental intervention research typically involves several tests of the intervention with modifications following each test.

A Definition

Developmental intervention research (DIR) involves the conceptualization, design, and on-going modifications of materials that go into creating applied social service programs, assessment and evaluation tools, polices, and direct service interventions, all of which can be classified as forms of interventions (Gilgun & Sands, 2012). DIR assumes that academic researchers partner with practitioners and often with members of target populations to craft interventions.

Another assumption is that DIR is a two-way street. Academic researchers bring knowledge to the field and practitioners in the field as well as members of target communities bring knowledge to academic researchers. Often DIR involves participatory action research, where academic researchers, professionals, and persons who are members of target groups work together to formulate action plans. Personal experiences and personal and professional values of all who craft interventions/programs/action plans also contribute to DIR.

The developers of intervention research, who are Rothman and Thomas (1994), hoped that it would bridge the gap between academic research and practice of various types. They also were responding to various other concerns of their time, such whether social work practice is effective and the desirability of practitioner contribution to the knowledge base through practice evaluation (Fraser & Galinksy, 2010; Thomas, 1978). These issues remain to this day.

Components

According to Rothman and Thomas (1994), DIR has three components:

1. **Knowledge Development (KD),** which they mean as the development of applied knowledge. Although Rothman and Thomas appear to exclude basic research, sometimes basic research is also part of the knowledge that individuals apply to interventions. This is so in translational research that takes basic scientific

knowledge like that related to DNA and applies it to many kinds of interventions/clinical uses.

2. **Knowledge Utilization (RU),** which is not well explained in Rothman and Thomas (1994), is a term that is used in many disciplines, including social work. The term typically means the identification and synthesis of basic and applied research and developing procedures, policies, programs, and other interventions that puts the research to practical use. Synthesis and applications is often called translational research (Translational research, n.d.). To do RU, persons who develop intervention use a wide variety of types of knowledge including research, theory and professional know-how. In addition, the knowledge is of the situation to be changed as well as the interventions meant to change it. For applied social work programs to work, the situations to be changed have to be understood by the persons for whom the intervention is crafted.

The project may also involve the modification of existing interventions to fit new populations.

3. **Design and Development (D & D)**, which is a complex, is composed of six parts. Its procedures incorporate the idea that design and development involves partnerships between researchers on social work faculties and practitioners in the field and often members of target populations. Although they are listed sequentially, developers move back and forth between all of the stages. D & D can take years.

Throughout the process of D & D, developers want to identify causal factors; that is factors that lead to good and poor outcomes. Often developers don't know for if the factors are causal but they can show that certain factors are associated with certain outcomes. For example, positive parental engagement in programming for their children who have problematic issues and their support of children's positive engagement consistently show better outcomes than when parents are disengaged and/or undermine their children's positive engagement. Maxwell's (2004) discussion shows many of the issues involved in identifying causal factors.

In addition, developers of interventions target issues that appear to have possibility of change, what Fraser and Galinsky (2010) call " **potentially malleable mediators**" (p. 461). What they mean is that factors such as parental positive engagement is a mediator between children's problematic issues and positive changes in those issues.

The phases of D & D are the following.

1. **Problem Analysis & Project Planning**. Problem analysis includes a formal or informal needs assessment, a review of relevant research and theory, discussions with knowledgeable professionals, and explications of developers' own practical and possibly theoretical knowledge. Project planning involves feasibility studies and goal setting.

The term *problem* is problematic. As Fraser and Galinksy (2010) point out, the specification of the issues involves not only the delineation of the negatives in a problematic situation but also the possible protective factors (factors that potentially could offset negatives. Perhaps the term *problematic situation* is more suitable.

2. **Information Gathering & Synthesis**. Although not totally clear in Rothman and Thomas (1994), this part of intervention/model development appears to be an extension of problem analysis and project planning. It involves elaboration of the problem—which is an unfortunate term—through more review of research and theory, consultations with professionals, and explications of developers' knowledge as well as thorough search for relevant interventions.

3. **Design of the Project.** This is complex and requires extensive training in research methods and design as well as skills in gaining entrée into field settings, recruitment, retention, and ethical issues.

4. **Early Development & Pilot Testing.** The assumption here is that the intervention will undergo changes and possibly many tests before and if there is a randomized controlled trial (RTC).

5. **Field Test.** To do field tests, developers recruit a large sample in order to create equivalent groups, which requires relatively large samples and randomization. Randomization means that the members of one large group have an equal chance to be part of the intervention group or one or more control groups. Randomization does not mean random samples. The groups are equivalent but not random that is they are not representative of a larger population. They represent only themselves. Relatively large groups are required in order to meet the assumptions related to the power of statistical tests.

When the treatment and control groups are equivalent, this design is called an experiment. When the groups are not equivalent, the design is called a quasi-experiment. The general working hypothesis of experiments and quasi-experiments is that the intervention caused outcome.

Internal validity—causation—can be demonstrated as strong in randomized studies but the external validity—generalizability—is no different from any other finding. Findings have to be tested for fit on other individuals and on other groups. Studies with equivalent groups are called randomized controlled groups. If the interveners do not know which groups received the intervention and which did not these are blind controlled trials.

Blind randomized controlled trials (RCT) are possible in medicine but unlikely in social work. Recruitment of groups large enough for RCTs is difficult for social work. The ethics of withholding an intervention requires much thought, but a delay in implementing the intervention for the control group is one way to get around that. These are called wait groups. Also, multiple baseline designs can get around some ethical issues.

Group designs as in experimental and quasi-experimental designs average out individual responses to interventions. Therefore qualitative studies of individuals can be helpful to identify some of the individual differences. Also there are hypotheses that compete with the hypothesis that the intervention caused the change. Developers have to identify and rule out or rule in competing hypothesis. Finally, measurement is a big issue. Developers have to ensure that their measurements actually capture what happens as a result of the intervention. Researchers also have to ensure that their use of statistical test is adequate. They may arrive at false negatives or false positives if their statistical analyses are incorrect or their sample is smaller than test require.

Whether an experiment or quasi-experiment, issues of other factors that cause outcome (competing/rival hypotheses), adequacy of measurement, and issues related to generalizability require attention.

Discussion

There are three dimensions to DIR: KD, KU, & D & D. D & D integrates the first two. Knowledge of persons and situations are integral to effective interventions. D & D is complex and can take years. Sometimes researchers do not get to a field test that involves RCT. Understanding what DIR is helps social work researchers understand where their own research fits with social work's applied mission.

References

Fraser, Mark W., & Maeda J. Galinsky (2010). Steps in intervention research: Designing and developing social programs. *Research on Social Work Practice, 20*, 459-466.

Gilgun, Jane F. & Roberta G. Sands (2012). The contributions of qualitative approaches to developmental intervention research. *Research on Social Work Practice, 11(4)*, 349-361.

Maxwell, Joseph (2004). Using qualitative methods for causal explanation. *Field Methods, 16*, 243-264.

Patton, Michael (2011). *Developmental evaluation: Applying complexity concepts to enhance innovation and use.* New York: Guilford.

Thomas, Edwin J. & Jack Rothman (1994). An integrative perspective on intervention research. In Jack Rothman & Edwin J. Thomas (Eds.), *Intervention research: Design and development for human services* (pp. 3-23). New York: Haworth.

Thomas, Edwin J. (1978) Mousetraps, developmental research, and social work education. *Social Service Review, 52(3)*, 468–483.

Translational Research (n.d.). Washington, DC: National Institutes of Health. IH Medical Research Scholars Program Retrieved September 18, 2012. http://commonfund.nih.gov/clinicalresearch/overview-translational.aspx

University of Minnesota, Twin Cities, USA
School of Social Work
SW 8861 Theory & Model Building
in Social Work
Jane F. Gilgun, Ph.D., LICSW

Checklist: Fitting Research Interests
into Developmental Intervention Research (DIR)

This is a worksheet for a PhD-level course in theory and model development. The purpose of the exercise is to guide students through an application of the ideas related to developmental intervention research (DIR). DIR is a set of procedures intended to bring the best we know to applications that are intended to improve quality of life in specified domains, such as gender identity, parenting, and promotion of the interests of persons with limited access to economic, social, spiritual, and artistic opportunities.

Intervention Knowledge Development (KD)

My project is
___ applied research
___ basic research
___ One of its purposes is to contribute to research and theory on human development.
___ Another of its purposes is to contribute to interventions: inform the general public, policy makers, direct practice, advocacy and policy, programs.
___ Its research methods are typical of social and behavioral sciences and also of the human sciences.
___ The results are descriptive material, concepts, empirical generalizations, hypotheses and/or theories.

___ Its audiences are others who also build knowledge in your area of interest as well as people who connect the knowledge to various interventions/practical applications.

Knowledge Utilization (KU)

___ The procedures of my project synthesize basic and applied research into procedures, policies, programs, and interventions; this is called translational research.

___ Its procedures involve the study of interventions/practical applications already created in order to develop additional interventions; sometimes called synthesis. *Caveat:* Important to include and take into consideration research, theory, and other knowledge about the situations and persons for whom the practice applications are intended .

___ The project may also involve the modification of existing interventions to fit new populations.

Design and Development (D & D)

___ My project modifies exiting technologies or develops new ones, such as intervention programs, treatment modalities, assessment tools.

___ Its procedures incorporate the idea that design and development involves exchanges between researchers on social work faculties and practitioners in the field.

___ It follows all or part of the six stages of D & D:

    ___ problem analysis & project planning

        ___ problem analysis: begin lit review, talk with experts, write down practice experience, do a needs assessment

    ___ project planning: feasibility & goals

    ___information gathering & synthesis

        ___ elaboration and finalization of problem analysis

    ___ design of the project (This is complicated.)

___ early development & pilot testing (may be multiple iterations)

___ field test—quasi-experiments and RCTs, both with qualitative components

___ dissemination

References

Thomas, Edwin J. & Jack Rothman (1994). An integrative perspective on intervention research. In Jack Rothman & Edwin J. Thomas (Eds.), Intervention research: Design and development for human services (pp. 3-23). New York: Haworth.

Translational Research (n.d.). Washington, DC: National Institutes of Health. IH Medical Research Scholars Program Retrieved 9.18. 12 http://commonfund.nih.gov/clinicalresearch/overview-translational.aspx

Characteristics of Social Work Research

Jane F. Gilgun, PhD, LICSW
Professor, School of Social Work
University of Minnesota, Twin Cities, USA

- **Values**
    - ○ Social justice, economic justice, social change, social reform
    - ○ Do no harm
    - ○ Dignity and worth of individual, self-determination
        - ▪ Reflexivity
            - • Researchers'
            - • Service users'
        - ▪ Advocacy
            - • Take into account the points of view of multiple others
            - • Clarity about one's own points of view
        - ▪ Immersion
            - • To understand multiple perspectives
                - ○ Multiple methods
                    - ▪ Not necessarily in each research project
        - ▪ Multiple methods—not necessary for each research project
            - • To understand social phenomena, to understand change processes, and to anticipate and understand consequences
        - ▪ Models that represent complexity

46

- **Person environment interactions**
  - Recognize the complex influences on human development, actions, and motivations (interests)
  - Recognize the inseparability of person from environments in the present and in the past
    - Key question: Do people internalize their experiences that become inner working models of what they expect of themselves, others, and how the world works?
  - Multiple methods—not necessary for each research project
    - Models that represent complexity

- **Centrality of Relationships for Understanding and for Change**
  - Common factors model
  - Social works' traditional emphasis on relationships—e.g. Perlman & others

- **Focus on interventions (causation)**
  - Variable-centered causations
  - Process-centered causations
  - Causal processes may be
    - naturally-occurring
    - experimenter manipulated
  - is there a cause and effect relationship between our interventions and our outcomes? What else might cause the outcomes? (internal validity)
  - Construct validity—does our theory of change in our models of practice match the processes and outcomes of our interventions? In other words, how do our hypothesized patterns of change match the patterns of change we observe?

- notions of intervening or confounding variables in relationship to what the causal factors are in interventions (constuct validity of design)
  - common factors model: significance of external influences
- adequate measures of processes and outcomes (construct validity of design)

- **Focus on model development or how things work**
  - General phenomena in need of models
    - Assessments: based on understanding target persons' experiences
    - Interventions: best estimate of what would work with particular persons, at particular times, under particular circumstances these persons, at this
    - Evaluations: what outcomes can we expect, how do we evaluate outcomes?

- **Models that suit social work**
  - Process Models
    - Common factors model
    - PAR/CBPR
    - Logic models
    - Task analysis
    - Deductive qualitative analysis
    - Grounded theory
    - Four cornerstones of EBP
    - Life histories/narrative analysis
  - Variable-centered models
    - Structural equation modeling
    - Multiple level modeling
    - Logistic regression
    - Etc.

- Hybrid models
  - Growth mixture modeling
  - Semi-parametric group-based modeling
  - Latent class analysis

Developing and Writing up Social Work-Specific Models of Practice

Jane F. Gilgun
University of Minnesota, Twin Cities, USA

Jane F. Gilgun, Ph.D., LICSW, is a professor, School of Social Work, University of Minnesota, Twin Cities, USA.
December 3, 2010.

Abstract

This detailed handout describes principles of social science writing for social workers and members of allied disciplines who want to develop, adapt, or analyze models of practice. Written primarily in outline form, the handout integrates critical thinking skills with procedures for developing models of practice. The handout also provides a structure for writing up the results of a model development, adaptation, or analysis project. A central premise of model development is the importance of knowing that models are incomplete but the best we can do at the time. We implement these models and carefully observe how they work or do not work. We then modify the models in light of what we learn through the implementation. We then implement the revised model and follow the same procedures. The basic value is to do no harm. The hope is to promote individual and social good. The basic principles are conjectures, refutations, and reformulations.

Developing and Writing up Social Work-Specific Models of Practice
Jane F. Gilgun, PhD, LICSW
2010

This handout summarizes guidelines discussed throughout the semester for the final project in the course, Theory and Model Building in Social Work. The final project involves the development, adaptation, and/or analysis of one or more models of practice. This handout integrates principles that are part of the course and the structure of research reports that is standard in the 6th edition of the *Publication Manual of the American Psychological Association*.

Students can adapt these guidelines to fit their specific projects. As discussed in class, however, certain features are required, such as demonstration of critical thinking skills, an analysis of a model using a social-work specific framework, and having a final section that is a summary, discussion, and reflection. The project represents opportunities to demonstrate their abilities to understand, integrate, and apply course learnings to one or more models of practice. This handout cannot cover every situation students will need to deal with. Students therefore will have to think about some things independently of this handout, change the order of some of the topics, add new areas to cover, and perhaps omit some of the non-required topics.

Demonstrate Critical Thinking Skills

Social science writing involves critical thinking skills, such as

- Logical organization of ideas
- Documentation of main ideas
- Clarity
- Directness
- Even-handedness—represent the points of views of others well
- Synthesis (or integration) of ideas from two or more sources
- Other relevant principles that are stated in writings about critical thinking skills

The following is a definition of critical thinking.

> Critical thinking is the intellectually disciplined process of actively and skillfully conceptualizing, applying, analyzing, synthesizing, and/or evaluating information gathered from, or generated by, observation, experience, reflection, reasoning, or communication, as a guide to belief and action. In its exemplary form, it is based on universal intellectual values that transcend subject matter divisions: clarity, accuracy, precision, consistency, relevance, sound evidence, good reasons, depth, breadth, and fairness

The authors of this statement are Michael Scriven & Richard Paul for the National Council for Excellence in Critical Thinking Instruction—available at the Foundation for Critical Thinking at http://www.criticalthinking.org/page.cfm?CategoryID=51 More information is in the course handout Critical Thinking in Writing Papers: Some Key Ideas.

In summary, critical thinking is an open-minded approach to building knowledge. It involves both processes of understanding multiple points of view about situations, ideas, and other people and then communicating these understandings in well-organized, clear, direct, and even handed ways. Critical thinking involves dialogue and leads to collaborations in order to bring multiple perspectives to bear on knowledge development.

Logical Organization of Ideas

Logical organization of ideas includes developing an overall structure for the paper and a clear logical flow of ideas.

The structure of the paper is based upon the guidelines in the 6th edition of the *APA Manual.* The four sections are

o Introduction
o Procedures
o Findings
o Discussion

As stated earlier, this handout modifies this structure slightly and changes some of the names of each section to fit the topic of the paper.

Logical organization of ideas includes the following. (See *APA Manual.*)

- A title that states the topic
- Writing in the first person ("I" or "we")
- An abstract/overview that summarizes the paper (See *APA Manual.*)
  - o Make it interesting
  - o Hooks & handles, if possible
- Topic is in the first sentence or soon afterward
- The first paragraph contains brief statements about the
  - o Topic

- Significance of topic
- How you developed the contents of the paper
- Potential or actual applications of the paper
- Directions researchers/practitioners/community members/policy makers/parents can go with the potential or actual findings
- Anything else authors believe is important

Introduction

The introduction to the paper includes the following in an order that authors decide fits the logic of their work. Authors can modify some of what goes into the paper depending upon the project, but for the present course authors must use a social work-specific framework to analyze the model and to justify its adaptation, if they are adapting it.

- The first paragraph as described above
- Description of the model(s) that are the subject of the project
- A literature review that is relevant to the model that is the subject of the paper
- Description of the social work-specific analytic framework that you use to analyze the model(s)
  - Some examples of sources of the analytic framework
    - Four Cornerstones
      - Service user and other user perspectives including values
      - Practitioner perspectives including personal and professional values & personal experience/reflective practice
      - Relevant research
      - Relevant theory
    - Common factors model

- Includes person in environment (PIE), relationships, motivations, skills, etc.
  - For example, does the model emphasize the importance of relationships and builds into the model relationship building, if the model has aspects that are interpersonal?

- Theories of change/causation, includes notions related to external influences, barriers to effectiveness even if the model is a good one, etc.
- Values related to social work
  - Tensions between values
  - Critical perspectives such as imbalances of power and how the model addresses them. Here "critical perspectives" refers to critical theory which focuses on power, its uses and misuses, as in critical race theory.
- Advocacy which is based upon values and an in-depth understanding of target populations' issues and how to address them
- Other models that help you construct a social work specific model of practice such as
  - PAR
  - Intervention research
  - Grounded theory
  - Task analysis, falsification, etc.

Procedures for Developing/Adapting/Analyzing a Model

- Description of the population for which your model is intended (Authors may have already described this population in the earlier section, if doing so made logical sense to them.)

Description of what you did in the development/adaptation/analysis (If you have not already described this.)
  - For example, how you analyzed model to see if it is social work-specific
- Descriptions of the heuristics you used that helped you think about components of your model, if you used them
- Anything else you did to develop/adapt/analyze the model, such as talking to other people, reflecting upon your experience, etc. Authors may already have covered this in an earlier section.

Procedures for Testing a Model

- Statement about the completeness of the model
- Statement about the varieties of outcomes you expect with some general ideas about the various conditions under which you will have the various outcomes
- Plans for documenting how the model works
  - Descriptions of change processes, positive negative, mixed that will result from implementation of the model
    - This can involve many different kinds of activities with anyone who has anything to do with the model of practice, such as observations, self-report, surveys, interviews, case record reviews, randomized controlled trials, quasi-experiments, etc;

- Plans for how you ensure that you will identify as many patterns of processes and outcomes as possible
    - Remember: one pattern/size does not fit all
    - Will you do negative case analysis—that is look for variety in your sampling— seek cases that do not fit your emerging descriptions?

- Plans for how you will adapt the model to fit how you have observed how it works
    - This is the feedback loop or the reformulation part of conjectures, refutations, and reformulation of models

Discussion

- Typically, this section begins with a summary.
- How authors interpret how the model works or may work, the strengths of the model, potential shortcomings
- Reflections upon
    - Expected outcomes
    - Expected applications
    - Future Directions
- Recommendations
- Any other thoughts authors have about the project
- Thoughts about significance of the findings/expected findings/applications/future directions

Discussion and Reflection for This Handout

This handout has provided guidelines for the final project in a social work theory and model building course. The project is an opportunity for students to demonstrate their mastery of course materials. This handout has integrated principles that are part of the course and the structure of research reports that is standard in the 6th edition of the *Publication Manual of the American Psychological Association.*

The development, analysis, and adaptation of models of practice are challenging. Doing this kind of work requires social workers to gather information from a variety of sources, to analyze the information, and then to synthesize the information. Constructing the model is a process that involves critical thinking skills. Authors are not done once they have constructed a model. They then must communicate in writing what they did in clear, direct, even-handed, and well-documented ways, once again following principles of critical thinking.

Selected References

American Psychological Association (2009). *Publication manual of the American Psychological Association* (6th ed.). Washington, DC: Author.

CSE's White Paper on Promoting Integrity in Scientific Journal Publications, 2009 Update, course handout

Gilgun, Jane F. (2010). Theory & Model-Building in Social Work: Course Syllabus

International Federation of Social Workers (2000). Definition of Social Work. Adopted by the IFSW General Meeting in Montréal, Canada, July 2000.

Gilgun, Jane F. (2010). *The NEATS: A Child & Family Assessment.* Available from the instructor and on Amazon.

Maxwell, Joseph (2004). Using qualitative methods for causal explanation. *Field Methods, 16,* 243-264

Pelton, Leroy H. (2001). Social justice and social work. *Journal of Social Work Education, 37(3),* 433-439.

Rolland, J.S. (2005). Cancer and the family: An integrative model. *Cancer,* 104(11sup), 2584-2595.

Smith-Maddox, Renee & Daniel G. Solorano (2002). Using critical race theory, Paulo Freire's problem-posing method, & case study research to confront race and racism in education. *Qualitative Inquiry, 8(1),* 66-84.

Wendt-Hironimus, Robert J. & Lora Ebert Wallace (2009). The sociological imagination and social responsibility. *Teaching Sociology, 37,* 76-78.

Preliminary Studies, Hypothesis Testing, and Qualitative Research
By Jane F. Gilgun
April 2003

When considering a study using qualitative methods, it is important to do preliminary exploration of your topic. Besides reading about your topic, you can do this through talking to knowledgeable people, such as friends, professionals, and others who have some experience with your topic. A preliminary study is probably necessary for proposal writing, in particular proposals you are planning to submit for funding. Strauss (1987) was explicit about this. He wrote, "No proposal should be written without preliminary data collection and analysis" (p. 286).

If you do preliminary studies, you will develop a focus, which is essential early in qualitative research, even though the purpose of many projects is to develop new understandings. In addition, preliminary studies will help you formulate questions that are stated in language that your informants will understand and experience as natural. Few dissertation committees will allow PhD students to procedure with their research without a clear conceptual framework and carefully stated research goals and procedures. Preliminary studies are necessary to do this. Finally, institutional review boards that oversee the ethical component of research will not approve studies that are vague in purpose, focus, and procedures.

The notion of preliminary studies is consistent with the work of Glaser and Strauss (1967). On the one hand, Glaser and Strauss recommended entering the field with no hypotheses to test and to see what emerges. This leads many researchers new to qualitative research to assume that these methodologists are stating that it is unnecessary to do prior literature reviews and to plan out research

62

procedures before the study begins. On the other hand, Glaser and Strauss also acknowledged in a footnote that researchers are not blank slates and bring their pre-conceptions with them.

Elizabeth Bott (1957) may have been one of the inspirations for Glaser and Strauss's (1967) thinking. She and her research team identified and elaborated upon the notion of social network through entering the field with no hypotheses to test. Yet, Bott also stated that her general conceptual framework was Lewin's ecological theory, which sensitized her to the notion of social networks. Schatzman (in Gilgun, 1993) discussed a similar phenomenon when a research team headed by Anselm Strauss identified and elaborated the term "negotiated order" (Strauss et al, 1964).

Thus, qualitative research may well begin with no hypotheses to test but as soon as researchers identify concepts and processes that they want to elaborate, they engage in a kind of testing. Glaser and Struass (1967) call this the constant comparative method, where they compare their findings within and across cases and modify their hypotheses to fit their findings. They identify new cases through theoretical sampling, which involves choosing cases on the basis of the promise they hold to elaborate upon or refine their emerging findings.

Constant comparison and theoretical sampling are similar to procedures of analytic induction, which begins with a conceptual model, sometimes simply a rough hypothesis or hunch based on intuition, and then seeks to test and elaborate upon this conceptual model. Analytic induction tests and develops new hypotheses and conceptual models through negative case analysis, a procedure that directs researchers to seek cases that may undermine emerging findings. If the new cases do this, the conceptual model is reformulated and modified.

In this way, researchers develop findings that are account for general patterns and exceptions. Since few qualitative studies have random samples, qualitative findings can tell us little or anything about prevalence but it can tell us a great deal about variations in patterns and meanings. Finally, analytic induction is not "pure" induction, just as grounded theory is not (Gilgun, 2002).

Students and new researchers often are confused about the place of prior hypotheses in qualitative research. It is little wonder. Major figures such as Glaser and Strauss (1967; Strauss & Corbin, 1998) are unclear. In the final analysis, preliminary studies are good practice, with full acknowledgement that researchers' prior notions shape their views of which phenomena are important. Once researchers identify the focus of their research, they are then positioned to do a literature review, develop a conceptual framework, set out goals of their research, and plan procedures of data collection and analysis.

Negative case analysis, which involves the conscious choosing of cases that will force modification and sometimes even refutation of emerging findings, is key to qualitative analysis. Many new researchers are tempted to see only what their conceptual models says is important. By directing researchers to seek material that will challenge their models, researchers are positioned to develop new understandings. It's easy to find material that supports prior frameworks. The skill of qualitative analysis is to challenge prior understandings so new meanings can emerge.

References

Bott, Elizabeth (1957). *Family and social network.* New York: Free Press. Second edition published in 1971.

Gilgun, Jane F. (2002). Conjectures and refutations: Governmental funding and qualitative research. *Qualitative Social Work, 1(3)*, 359-375.

Gilgun, Jane F. (1993). Dimensional analysis and grounded theory: An interview with Leonard Schatzman. *Qualitative Family Research, 7 (1 &2)*, 1-2, 4-7.

Popper, Karl R. (1969). *Conjectures and refutations: The growth of scientific knowledge.* London: Routledge and Kegan Paul.

Strauss, Anselm (1987). *Qualitative analysis for social scientists.* New York: Cambridge University Press.

Strauss, Anselm, & Juliet Corbin (1998). *Basics of qualitative research: Techniques and procedures for developing grounded theory* (2nd ed.). Thousand Oaks, CA: Sage.

Strauss, Anselm, Leonard. Schatzman, Rue Bucher, Danuta Ehrlich, & Marvin Sabshin (1964). *Psychiatric ideologies and institutions.* New York: Free Press.

Jane F. Gilgun, Ph.D., LICSW, is professor, School of Social Work, University of Minnesota, Twin Cities, 1404 Gortner Avenue, St. Paul, MN 55108. Phone: 612/624-3643; fax: 612/624-3744; e-mail: jgilgun@umn.edu.

**Guidelines for Doing
a Task Analysis**

- First, write your theory of the processes of how clients change.

- Second, observe how clients in your practice actually do change, if they do.

- Third, compare your theory to your observations of how clients changed in this one case.

- Fourth, change your original theory to fit this case.

- Fifth, describe how these processes of change relate to outcome.

- Sixth, test your model on the next case.

University of Minnesota, Twin Cities, USA
School of Social Work
SW 8861 Theory & Model Building in Social Work
Jane F. Gilgun, PhD, LICSW
Fall 2012

Methods of Theory Development

1. "Arm-chair theorizing" that can be based upon
   - Observations and reflections
   - Reflections upon personal experiences
   - Combinations of the above
     - common way of theorizing, especially for philosophers and theoreticians earlier in the 20th century including Parsons, Bacon, Descartes, and many others
     - possible that economists and members of other disciplines continue to do this kind of theorizing
   - Synthesis of existing research and theory to formulate a more comprehensive theory
     - Family scholars in the in the middle of the 20th century made such efforts; Ruben Hill was a catalyst for this kind of theorizing
     - Theoretical frameworks used to provide concepts and theories put to use in research projects are forms of arm-chair theories.

2. Starting with a theory and attempting to elaborate upon It
   - Initial theories can be "arm-chair theories" developed in the ways discussed earlier. Researchers use these initial theories in a comparative way. They compare the theory with patterns they find through empirical research.

- Researchers change the theories according to the patterns they identify through their empirical research.
- Task analysis, analytic induction, and deductive qualitative analysis are approaches of this type.

These theories are forever open to modification.

3. Approaches Based on Enthographic Styles
Researchers begin with no theory to test or elaborate but they typically use sensitizing concepts that guide them in their procedures. Examples of sensitizing concepts are assumptions about importance of understanding persons in contexts, obtain multiple points of view in order to account for multiple perspectives, and the idea that researchers influence research processes.

Some but not all ethnographies have theories as their products, but are more focused on description, which is based upon concepts. Thus, descriptions have a theoretical component.

Grounded theory is a form of theory development that begins with no theory to test or elaborate but does have sensitizing concepts.

Definition of Theory

Theories are composed of one or more hypotheses. Hypotheses are statements of relationships between concepts. Concepts are clearly defined both conceptually and operationally. When concepts are defined conceptually and operationally, they are useful to researchers because researchers can show links between the concepts and the concrete indicators of concepts that researchers observe in their interviews, observations, and documents.

References

Berlin, Sharon B., Katherine B. Mann, & Susan F. Grossman, (l991). Task analysis of cognitive therapy for depression. *Social Work Research & Abstracts, 27 (2)*, 3-11.

Gilgun, Jane F. (2005). Qualitative research and family psychology. *Journal of Family Psychology,19(1)*, 40-50.

Rolland, J.S. (2005). Cancer and the family: An integrative model. *Cancer*, 104(11sup), 2584-2595.

White, James M. (2012). The current status of theorizing about families. In Gary W. Peterson & Kevin R. Bush (Eds.), *Handbook of marriage and the family* (3rd ed.) (pp. 11-37). New York: Springer.

University of Minnesota, Twin Cities
School of Social Work
SW 8861 Theory and Model Building in Social Work
Jane F. Gilgun, PhD, LICSW
Fall 2012

Theory & Model Building in Social Work:
Synthesis & Integration of Ideas

Assignment for Tuesday, November 20, 2012

We are not meeting on the Tuesday, November 20, which is a few days before Thanksgiving. I would like you to take the time off to reflect upon the topics we have covered in this course, draw principles from these topics, and reflect upon how these principles are relevant to theory and model-building in social work in general and to your possible course project in particular. This assignment will help you to prepare in a systematic way for your final projects. It is a step toward building a framework that you will use to analyze a theory or model or that you will use to build a theory or model.

As a reminder, I described the final project in the syllabus as

Final project, 40 points. This final project is your opportunity to show that you can apply course learnings to theory and model building. In this assignment, you can

- analyze an existing model of practice and/or theory relevant to social work;
- modify an existing model of practice or theory;
- create a new model of practice or put together a new theory of practice for a particular domain and show how you will test the model or theory.

The theories and models of practice that you work with in this assignment are likely to be "partial," meaning they focus on a particular aspect of practice, such as assessment, intervention, or evaluation, or involve testing a particular model of practice through task analysis, or involve an informed analysis of a method of theory-testing/theory-building. Length: up to 14 pages for sole authored papers and up to 20 pages for multiple-authored papers. Due Monday, December 17 at midnight.

Students may negotiate with the instructor another kind of final project. Students will present drafts of these final papers during the last two classes of the semester, which are classes 14 and 15, December 4 and 11.

My Suggestions

I suggest that you review one or more of the topics covered in the class. Read and reflect upon the readings I assigned for those topics. I also suggest that you search for other readings on the topics and read and reflect upon them. Then write down principles related to theory and model building that you draw from these readings. For example, the four cornerstones material points out four sources of "evidence" for doing social work practice. Theory and model building are social work practices. A question to ask about a theory and/or model you are working with for your final project is, What are the sources of evidence that this theory or model has used? Does it use one or two or all four? Is the model trustworthy if it uses one or two sources or would it be more trustworthy if it used three or four sources? What suggestions do you have for creating a more trustworthy model? What do you mean by trustworthy?

Also, as we have said in class, a hallmark of theory and model building is that they are under continual development. We are currently learning about theory development. Principles that can be drawn from these readings and discussions include whether there is a discernable theory of change in the model or theory, whether the practice of the theory or the model includes a search for "evidence" or findings that do not fit the current theory of change, and whether there are procedures in place where practitioners can discuss how the model/theory works and whether the model/theory requires revision.

During this time of reflection on course learnings, you might also want to think about whether there are common ideas across course topics. For example, does developmental intervention research have anything in common with the common factors model, the four cornerstones idea, logic models, and theory development? You would first have to have a good understanding of each of these topics, and you would also have to have written down some of the principles from each of these topics. Then you can do the comparisons across topics. This is synthesis, which is a central skill in scholarship.

In addition, you can reflect upon whether ideas from each of the topics complement ideas from other topics. For example, what if anything does developmental intervention research cover that the common factors model does not? What does the common factors model cover that developmental intervention research does not? How do ideas from these two topics complement each other? What other topics complement the emerging integration of ideas?

Although for the purposes of this assignment, I suggest that you do this kind of analysis with one or two topics, for the final project, I expect you to apply each of the course topics to your final project and to show that you can synthesize ideas (connect common ideas) and integrate ideas (show their complementary) in the framework you use for your final project.

Some Guidelines for Structure of the Final Project

Thinking ahead, the broad framework for your final project would be composed minimally, a description of the project, a description of the framework you used to analyze or build a model or theory, a description of how you applied the framework in your analysis or theory/model development, the results of the application, and a discussion. There may be other topics that are important to cover in the final project.

University of Minnesota, Twin Cities
School of Social Work
Jane F. Gilgun, Ph.D., LICSW
November 2012

Guidelines for Oral Presentations:
What's Your Point?
by Bob Boylan
as summarized by Jane Gilgun

"The ability to express an idea is nigh
as important as an idea itself."
Bernard Baruch

Good presentations are
- clear and concise
- lead to actions on the part of your audience—or at least a change in thinking

Presenters

- can handle situations that come up—like awkward question, AV equipment does work
- presents self as someone with authority—but still open to new perspectives.

Note: most people are afraid to do public presentation—many more afraid of dying than of doing public presentations

Skills needed
- eye contact
- calm, relaxed
- good use of body language
- vocal energy
- story telling

together with
- organization
- preparation

Audience analysis
- How many
- What is their preparation for/knowledge of the topic
- How receptive will they be to what you want to say?
- Answer the question that audience members have: What's in it for me?
- Types of audience
  - respectful
  - neutral
  - hostile, resistant, or defensive
    - admit the difference
    - present the other's favorable arguments
    - appeal to opponents sense of fairness—more likely to hear you if s/he believes you have heard him/her
  - setting
    - get there early
    - check that everything works/set up well
      - a desk/podium can be a barrier between you and audience

note: assume that even if audience is knowledgeable, they will want to know how you see things

The content is
- focused
  - Who are you addressing?
  - What do you want to say?

- o What are the benefits to audiences?

  - Correct
  - You believe in it

- What do you want to say?
  - What is your point of view?
    - o Does it make sense?
    - o Do you believe it?
    - o Is it the essence of what you want to say?
    - o Does it have some benefit to the audience?
    - o Are you committed to it
    - o Is it as concise as it can be?
  - What are your main points?
    - o What supports your main points?
      - Personal/professional experiences
      - Experiences of others you can tell first-hand
      - Research
      - Theory
  - Points to remember
  - Therefore, I recommend or I plan to do the following....

Reference

Boylan, Bob. What's your point?
http://www.amazon.com/Whats-Your-Point-Bob-Boylan/dp/158062460X

Guidelines for Responses
to Oral Presentations:
Dignity & Respect as Basic Values

By Jane F. Gilgun, Ph.D., LICSW

While there are some guidelines for presenting material in teaching and training and at scholarly conferences (Boylan, 1988; Jaccard & Jacoby, 2010), there is less guidance for how audiences respond to presentations in helpful ways. This paper outlines some guidelines for constructive conversations between presenters and members of audiences.

The basic principle is for audience members to respect the efforts that presenters have made to find the information, to shape it into presentations, and then to do the presentations. Presenters, too, must be respectful of audience members' constructive comments.

People present information to audiences for many different reasons, typically because they have information they want to share and sometimes because they would like audience members' thoughts about the information and presenting style. Some types of responses that presenter want are the following.

Clarification: Presenters may have specialized knowledge that audience members may not have. In those cases, it is helpful to presenters if audience members ask questions to clarify points that may be unclear. In *Roberts' Rules of Order*, for example, the standard practice is that clarifying questions have priority. The audience member says, "Mr. Speaker, point of information." The speaker acknowledges the request for information, and then the audience member states the question. Everything stops so that audience members can get the information from presenters.

What works. Presenters want to know what they did well and what could add to the points they have made.

Logic of the presentation. Presenters often like to know if their presentations are logical. Do the parts of the presentation fit together? Are the points well-supported? Is the presentation clear? Start with what presenters did well.

Did you hear me? Presenters typically welcome comments such as the above, but they may find it difficult to respond when audience members talk about what is present in their own minds but is not part of what the presenters actually said. Be sure you understand the points presenters are making. You might even repeat one or two of them before you speak.

The following are other guidelines for responding to presentations. Following them will help make the experience constructive for the presenters and for the audiences.

- **Use principles of critical thinking**
  - As a respondent to presentations
    - represent the points of views of presenters fairly
    - document your own perspectives with examples
    - speak in simple, clear language

- **Analyze the presentation by thinking about**
  - the basis of the presenter's points
  - claims the presenters making
  - whether the presenters' points are well-documented

o   what you want: Do you want some clarification that will make the presenters' points clear?—this is not to make your own points or to "score" against the presenter.
o   whether the presenter want from the audience
o   whether you can add anything to the points the presenter is making
o   whether you can be helpful

o   **Offer alternatives** that may add to the number of factors related to particular situations: e.g., many different reasons that account for career successes; many different responses to sexual assaults

o   **Avoid weak arguments** as defined in theories of rhetoric
  o   No *ad hominem* attacks—personal attacks
  o   No *argumentum ad populum*—every one believes it and so it must be true
  o   Don't change the subject or divert the topic to another
  o   No arguing from ignorance—because you haven't heard of it doesn't mean that someone else might not have a knowledge claim

References

Boylan, Bob (1988). *What's your point?* Wayzata, MN: Point Publications.

Jacard, James & Jacob Jacoby (2010). *Theory construction and model-building skills: A practical guide for social scientists.* New York: Guilford.

Social Marketing & Social Work:
An Example Using Promotion of Well-Being
as a Strategy to Reduce Violence

by Jane Gilgun

Summary

This article shows the usefulness of social marketing. Rather than selling toothpaste or a new car for profit, social marketing involves selling people on behaviors that will promote their health and well-being. Sometimes social marketing efforts seeks to influence the good of societies as well. Through a proposed campaign to reduce violence, this article shows the strategies of social marketing. Social marketing and social work are a natural fit.

About the Author

Jane Gilgun is a professor, School of Social Work, University of Minnesota, Twin Cities, USA. For many years, Jane has done research on the meanings of violence to perpetrators, the development of violent behaviors, and how persons overcome adversities. See Jane's other articles, books, and children's stories on scribd.com, Amazon, iBooks, Barnes & Noble, and other booksellers.

Social Marketing & Social Work:
An Example Using Promotion of Well-Being
as a Strategy to Reduce Violence

Social marketing is a strategy for fostering change in people's beliefs and behaviors. Rather than selling products to make money as in regular marketing, social marketing aims to promote individual and social good. An example of a social marketing campaign is the education of parents and professionals about the importance of fluids when infants and young children have diarrhea. If parents do not help children replenish fluids, they may die from dehydration, often within a few hours. Maintaining health is another way of thinking about preventing deaths through dehydration.

I am interested in preventing violence. Promoting individual and social well-being is another way of thinking about the prevention of violence. In my 30 years of doing interview research on violence, I have never met anyone who committed violence while experiencing a sense of well-being.

The purpose of this article is to explore social marketing as a strategy for promoting individual and social well-being by seeking to reduce and prevent acts of violence in families, communities, and within and among nations.

Social marketing and social work research are a natural fit. Social work research is rarely done only because the topic is interesting but also because researchers want to bring about individual, social, and structural change, consistent with such values as social and economic justice, respect for the dignity, worth, and self-determination of individuals, and the importance of relationships. In addition, prevention is emerging as a practice area in social work. Social marketing provides a set of strategies that social workers can use in their efforts to prevent the occurrence of social problems.

The Four P's

Social marketing campaigns are constructed from the Four P's: product, price, place, and promotion. Social marketers consult with members of target groups to develop the product, and they usually return to target groups once they have crafted the message, the price, the place, and the promotion. I define and discuss each of thee terms later in this article. Besides the big four, social marketers often strategize about audiences, partnerships, and paying for the campaign itself.

Product

In social marketing, the product is the message that the campaign wants to convey. Social marketers conduct research in order to discover how the targets of campaigns think about the issues and whether or not they believe actions are warranted. They talk to people, individually and in groups. The idea of consulting with targets of the campaign shows the importance of understanding what is important to them and starting from there. In addition, these individuals often have ideas about how to craft the messages and how and where to publicize the campaign.

I have done in-depth interview research on violence for more than 30 years with more than 160 people. Thirty-one of these interviews were for the purposes of constructing a social marketing campaign to persuade perpetrators of child sexual abuse and persons thinking of sexually abusing children to turn themselves in.

I have learned that for persons who perpetrate, various types of violence are exciting, thrilling, and fulfilling. Violence can restore honor and prove you've got guts. For sex-based violence, the experience can be blissful and romantic. Some persons have stated that they get no pleasure out of violence but felt pressured into committing it. This pressure can involve fear of getting hurt themselves if they do not commit violent acts and expediency in terms of solving a problem.

A few men told me that threats against their own lives compelled them to harm others. A man who had been in the US Army refused to shoot women and children. His sergeant held a gun to his head and said, "Shoot. He did." An example of expediency is the drug dealer who murdered one of his distributors when the distributor kept the money rather than giving it to the dealer. From the dealer's point of view, he has to kill. If he doesn't others will do the same thing. Another example is the man who murdered his children to keep them from going into foster care. He knew he was going to prison because he had killed their mother, his fiancée and at least two other women.

At its core, violence solves problems for those who perpetrate. Feeling miserable? Sexually abuse a child or rape a woman. Feeling angry? Release the tension through verbal, physical, or sexual abuse. Want to get back at someone? Hurt them or someone they care about, like their mother or their child. Want to avoid being taken advantage of? Kill.

A social marketing campaign would be based squarely on these accounts. No matter the variations, the core issue appears to be how to solve a problem that is vexing.

From my point of view, these solutions to problems hurt many others and often end up hurting those who perpetrate. Many who commit violence feel remorse afterward. Many therefore show evidence of tunnel vision. They don't consider alternative actions and they don't consider the consequences of their actions for their targets, for themselves, and for those who care about targets and themselves.

What is the product, then?

A possible product would involve selling the idea that there are other ways of solving problems besides violence. The strategies that lead to other solutions besides violence include the consideration of alternatives and the consideration consequences of various alternatives. To consider alternatives, individuals often benefit from consulting with others to get ideas besides their own on possible courses of actions and consequences.

I'd like to incorporate a few other ideas into the product or message that the campaign will sell. These ideas include three related to being happy, which is another way of taking about well-being, more or less. These three ideas are people who are happy 1) have good relationships with other people, 2) manage their emotions well, 3) and have beliefs that promote their own well-being and the well-being of others. I developed these ideas through my long-term research on violence.

I am thinking that the product could be along the following lines.

- Bugged? Angry? Hurt? Afraid?
- Want to do something about it?
    - Turn to people you trust and talk to them.
    - Do something that takes your mind off things like a movie, or a sports event, or recreating you enjoy.
    - Think about what will happen if you do what you most want to do about being bugged, hurt, angry, or afraid.

Before I would settle on the product, however, I would return to target audiences for their views.

Price

The second P, price, involves considering what individuals would have to give up in order to accept and follow the messages of the campaign. This part of the planning for the campaign also involves considerations of what individuals will gain.

What people will lose is the rush of thinking about violent acts and actually committing them. For many who perpetrate, violence is the greatest feeling in the world and often goes to the core identities. This is a great deal to give up. There may not be this incredible rush when doing honest problem-solving.

What people may get from problem-solving is deep emotional pain and also a sense of peace that comes with dealing forthrightly with difficult issues.

So, another message would be

- It takes guts to talk to someone about things that really bug you.
- It takes guts to resist the rush.
- It takes a real man to tell the truth about themselves to other people.

Short-term gain or long-term happiness? It's your choice.

It's not easy, but it's worth it.

Place

The strategies related to place involve how does the product of the campaign reach targets? Interviews with target audiences are helpful here, too. On the other hand, violence is so pervasive that any place that people congregate could be places to convey the messages of the social marketing campaign.

In the promotion of individual and social well-being for the purposes of reducing violence, there are many potential places to do this. Here are some.

- Treatment programs
- School-based education programs
- Parenting programs
- Exchanges with medical providers
- Religious education programs
- Internet
- Television

Promotion

Promotion involves the specific media that the campaign will use. Here are some possibilities.

- Posters
- Brochures
- Billboards
- Public service announcements
- Testimonies of prominent people like well-known athletes
- Children's stories
- Games and puzzles
- Facebook pages
- Websites
- Videos on the internet

Various Publics

This part of the campaign involves strategizing about primary and secondary audiences. While everyone could benefit from reminders about how to promote their own well-being and the well-being of others, social marketers do have to think about the various audiences that require attention if their messages are to result in actions.

So, while persons in treatment programs for violence-related issues, parents and professionals, and children in various programs are likely primary audiences, policy-makers including school boards, legislators, and holders of appointed and elected offices are other audiences of interest. Enlisting them in the campaign would be foundation to the success of the campaign.

This part of the campaign would be directed to what they can do to support the promotion of the individual and social well-being—and problem-solving abilities--of those whom they influence.

Here's a sample.

Message to teachers: Got a minute? How about spending five minutes a day with students about problem solving? If you do that, you may reduce the problems in your own classroom and promote children's healthy functioning.

Message to legislators: Want to save money on social service entitlements? Fund a training for teachers during the fall education week on the promotion of student well-being through problem-solving.

Partnerships

Some issues, like the present issue, are complex and require partnerships. So far, I am the only one crafting this social marketing campaign. Who else might be interested? Here are some things I can do.

- Encourage PhD students to consider a social marketing campaign for their dissertations
- Talk to social service agency administrators about incorporating ideas from the campaign as well as asking them for more ideas about the campaign itself

- Talk to legislators and school boards about joining with the campaign
- Talk to other social workers about the campaign and its possibilities

Policy

This part of the campaign involves the crafting of proposals for polices and programs. The ideas of the present campaign would contribute to this. In addition, the partnerships with potential audiences and long-term effort will result in polices and programs that get implemented.

Paying for the Campaign

Important to social marketing is finding the money to pay for it. For the campaign under discussion, I can do a lot of it through the mass media such as various ways to use the internet and through my teaching and writing.

A more comprehensive campaign would involve writing a proposal and finding funders.

Discussion

Many people are seeking ways of dealing with the challenges in their lives. Social marketing campaigns promote ideas about how to deal with such challenges. Social marketing is based on the experiences of individuals who are dealing with the issues of concern. For this reason alone, social marketing has great potential. People change their beliefs and actions when they feel understood.

Social work and social marketing have a great deal in common. Both seek to promote the common good and are based upon values such as justice, care, and self-determination. Social marketing provides a set of procedures that fits well with already-established social work practices. It is not a big leap for social work professionals to routinely engage in social marketing campaigns, both large-scale and small-scale. Small-scale campaigns could involve efforts within a single agency, while large-scale campaigns could involve a community, a region, a state, a nation, or several nations.

References

Andreasen, Alan R. (2002). Marketing social marketing in the social change marketplace. Journal of Public Policy & Marketing, 21(1), 3-13.

Bloom, Paul N., & William D. Novelli (1981). Problems and challenges in social marketing. Journal of Marketing, 45 , 79-88.(2), 79-88.

Boehm, Amnon, & Haya Itzhaky (2004). The social marketing approach: A way to increase reporting and treatment of sexual assault. Child Abuse & Neglect, 28, 253-265.

Dearing, James W. Everett M. Rogers et al (1996). Social marketing and diffusion-based strategies for communicating with unique populations: HIV prevention in San Francisco. Journal of Health Communication, 1, 343-363.

Grier, Sonya, & Carol A. Bryant (2005). Social marketing in public health. Annual Review of Public Health, 26, 319-339.

Hertie, Marilyn & Garth W. Martin (2002). Knowledge diffusion in social work: A new approach to bridging the gap. Social Work, 47(1), 85-95.

Lens, Vicki (2004). Principled negotiation: A new tool for case advocacy. Social Work, 49(3), 506-513.

McKenzie-Mohr, Doug. (2000). Promoting sustainable behavior: An introduction to community-based social marketing. Journal of Social Issues, 5(3), 543-554.

McKenzie-Mohr, Doug. (2000) Fostering sustainable behavior through community-based social marketing. American Psychologist, 55(5), 531-537

Martin, G. W., M. A. Herie, B. J. Turner, & J. A. Cunningham (1998). A social marketing model for disseminating research-based treatments to addictions treatment providers. Addiction, 93(11), 1703-1715.

Pfieffer, James. (2204). Condom Social Marketing, Pentecostalism, and Structural Adjustment in Mozambique: A Clash of AIDS Prevention Messages. (2004). Medical Anthropology Quarterly, 18(1), 77-103.

Stoner, Madeline R. (1986). Marketing of social services gains prominence in social services. Administration in Social Work, 41-52.

ABOUT THE AUTHOR

Jane F. Gilgun, PhD, LICSW, is a professor, School of Social Work, University of Minnesota, Twin Cities, USA. She has used qualitative methods such as grounded theory and deductive qualitative analysis to develop many different theories and models, including the NEATS, the CASPARS, and the four cornerstones of evidence-based practice, and theories and models on the meanings of violence to perpetrators, on how persons overcome adversities, and on the development of violent behaviors. She has published widely in these areas.

She worked at a public Rhode Island child welfare social service agency for several years and then became a professor. She also writes children's books, non-fiction, and articles that are available on Amazon, iBooks, Barnes & Noble, Smashwords, and scribd.com for a variety of mobile devices. She has many videos on YouTube that include the landscapes in Northwest Ireland, trail riding in Minnesota and elsewhere, horse racing, pig racing, and more.

Her interests include her horses, Padron's Elegante (Ellie) and Finn MacCool, who are mother and son, her dog Jazz, gardening, photography, cooking, the arts, and spending time in County Leitrim and County Sligo, Ireland.

Jane has a bachelor's and master's in English and American poetry from the Catholic University of America and the University of Rhode Island, respectively, a master's in social work from the University of Chicago, a licentiate in family studies and sexuality from the Catholic University of Louvain, Belgium, and a Ph.D. in child and family studies from Syracuse University. She is a licensed independent clinical social worker.

www.ingramcontent.com/pod-product-compliance
Lightning Source LLC
Chambersburg PA
CBHW070551290526
45790CB00002B/640